Top 50 Most Delicious

Empanada Recipes

An Empanada Cookbook

by Graham Bourdain

Copyright © 2023 Graham Bourdain

All Rights Reserved

Disclaimer

Reasonable care has been taken to ensure that the information presented in this book is accurate. However, the reader should understand that the information provided does not constitute legal, medical or professional advice of any kind.

No Liability: this product is supplied "as is" and without warranties. All warranties, express or implied, are hereby disclaimed. Use of this product constitutes acceptance of the "No Liability" policy. If you do not agree with this policy, you are not permitted to use or distribute this product.

We shall not be liable for any losses or damages whatsoever (including, without limitation, consequential loss or damage) directly or indirectly arising from the use of this product.

Please note that the nutritional values may vary depending on the specific ingredients and measurements used, as well as the method of cooking.

It's always a good idea to consult a registered dietitian or use an online nutrition calculator to get the most accurate nutritional value for a recipe, based on the ingredients and measurements you use.

Table of Contents

1. Beef and Potato Empanadas

Prep: 15 min. Cook: 30 min. Ready in: 45 min. Servings: 6

Ingredients:

1 lb. beef, diced

2 medium potatoes, peeled and diced

1 onion, diced

2 cloves of garlic, minced

1 tsp paprika

1 tsp cumin

Salt and pepper to taste

4 tbsp of cilantro, chopped

4 tbsp of raisins (optional)

1 package of empanada dough (store-bought or homemade)

1 egg, beaten (for egg wash)

Cooking Directions:

Alright folks, listen up. This recipe is a classic and it's going to knock your socks off. Beef and Potato Empanadas, it's a combination of flavors that just can't be beat.

Let's start with the filling. Take a pan, throw in some diced beef, and brown it up real nice. Drain off any excess fat and add in some diced onions and minced garlic. Give it a good stir and let those onions sweat and caramelize. Now, add in some diced potatoes, it will bring a nice texture to this dish. Season that with some paprika, cumin, salt, and pepper, and you're on your way to flavor town.

Add in some raisins, if you like, it will give a nice contrast of sweet and savory. Remove from heat and let it cool down before you start assembling your empanadas.

Next, roll out your empanada dough. I like mine to be about 1/8 inch thick. Cut out some circles. Place a tablespoon of filling on one side of the dough circle. Brush the edges of the dough with the beaten egg. Fold the dough over the filling, forming a half-moon shape and press the edges to seal. Brush the top with the beaten egg. Place the empanadas on a baking sheet lined with parchment paper.

Pop those bad boys in the oven at 375F (190C) for 20-25 minutes or until golden brown. Serve 'em up nice and warm, maybe with some chimichurri or aji on the side.

And there you have it, folks. The perfect beef and potato empanadas. Savor it, and don't be shy with the hot sauce.

<u>Enjoy</u>

2. Chicken and Corn Empanadas

Prep: 15 min. Cook: 25 min. Ready in: 40 min. Servings: 6

Ingredients:

1 lb chicken breast, diced

2 cups of sweet corn

1 onion, diced

2 cloves of garlic, minced

1 red bell pepper, diced

1/4 cup of cilantro, chopped

Salt and pepper to taste

1 package of empanada dough (store-bought or homemade)

1 egg, beaten (for egg wash)

Cooking Directions:

Let's get our hands dirty, folks. This recipe is a classic and it's going to be a crowd-pleaser. Chicken and Corn Empanadas, a combination of flavors that just can't be beat.

In a pan, brown the chicken over medium-high heat. Drain the fat. Add in some diced onions and minced garlic. Give it a good stir and let those onions sweat and caramelize. Now, add in some sweet corn, it will bring a sweet crunch to this dish. Season that with some salt and pepper, and you're on your way to flavor town. Stir in some diced red bell pepper and chopped cilantro for some extra color and flavor. Remove from heat and let it cool down before you start assembling your empanadas.

Next, roll out your empanada dough. I like mine to be about 1/8 inch thick. Cut out some circles. Place a tablespoon of filling on one side of the dough circle. Brush the edges of the dough with the beaten egg. Fold the dough over the filling, forming a half-moon shape and press the edges to seal. Brush the top with the beaten egg. Place the empanadas on a baking sheet lined with parchment paper.

Pop those bad boys in the oven at 375F (190C) for 20-25 minutes or until golden brown. Serve 'em up nice and warm, maybe with some chimichurri or aji on the side.

And there you have it folks, the perfect chicken and corn empanadas. Savor it and have fun with the toppings.

Enjoy

3. Vegetable Empanadas

Prep: 15 min. Cook: 25 min. Ready in: 40 min. Servings: 4

Ingredients:

1 cup of diced mushrooms

1 cup of diced bell pepper

1/2 cup of diced onion

1/2 cup of diced carrot

1/2 cup of diced zucchini

1/4 cup of cilantro, chopped

Salt and pepper to taste

1 package of empanada dough (store-bought or homemade)

1 egg, beaten (for egg wash)

Cooking Directions:

Alright folks, listen up. This recipe is a classic and it's going to knock your socks off. Vegetable empanadas, it's a combination of flavors that just can't be beat.

In a pan, sauté the vegetables over medium-high heat until they are tender. Add in some diced onion, minced garlic, diced mushrooms, diced bell pepper, diced carrot, and diced zucchini. Give it a good stir and let those vegetables sweat and caramelize. Season that with some salt and pepper, and you're on your way to flavor town.

Add in some cilantro for some extra color and flavor. Remove from heat and let it cool down before you start assembling your empanadas. Next, roll out your empanada dough. I like mine to be about 1/8 inch thick. Cut out some circles. Place a tablespoon of filling on one side of the dough circle. Brush the edges of the dough with the beaten egg.

Fold the dough over the filling, forming a half-moon shape and press the edges to seal. Brush the top with the beaten egg. Place the empanadas on a baking sheet lined with parchment paper.

Pop those bad boys in the oven at 375F (190C) for 20-25 minutes or until golden brown. Serve 'em up nice and warm, maybe with some chimichurri or aji on the side.

And there you have it, folks. The perfect vegetable empanadas. Savor it, and don't be shy with the hot sauce.

Enjoy

4. Beef and Olive Empanadas

Prep: 15 min. Cook: 25 min. Ready in: 40 min. Servings: 4

Ingredients:

3/4 lb. ground beef

3/4 cup of green olives, chopped

1/2 onion, diced

1 1/2 cloves of garlic, minced

1/2 tsp of cumin powder

Salt and pepper to taste

3/4 package of empanada dough (store-bought or homemade)

3/4 egg, beaten (for egg wash)

Cooking Directions:

Listen up, folks. This recipe is a game-changer. Beef and Olive Empanadas, a combination of flavors that just can't be beat.

In a pan, brown the beef over medium-high heat. Add in some diced onion, minced garlic, and a teaspoon of cumin powder. Give it a good stir and let those aromatics release their flavors. Season that with some salt and pepper, and you're on your way to flavor town.

Add in some chopped green olives. Remove from heat and let it cool down before you start assembling your empanadas.

Next, roll out your empanada dough. I like mine to be about 1/8 inch thick. Cut out some circles. Place a tablespoon of filling on one side of the dough circle. Brush the edges of the dough with the beaten egg. Fold the dough over the filling, forming a half-moon shape and press the edges to seal.

Place the empanadas on a baking sheet lined with parchment paper. Brush the top with the beaten egg. Bake those bad boys in the oven at 375F (190C) for 20-25 minutes or until golden brown. Serve 'em up nice and warm, maybe with some chimichurri or aji on the side.

And there you have it folks, the perfect beef and olive empanadas.

Enjoy

5. Spinach and Feta Empanadas

Prep: 15 min. Cook: 20 min. Ready in: 35 min. Servings: 4

Ingredients:

1 cup of chopped spinach

1/2 cup of crumbled feta cheese

1/2 onion, diced

1 clove of garlic, minced

1/4 tsp of cumin powder

Salt and pepper to taste

3/4 package of empanada dough (store-bought or homemade)

3/4 egg, beaten (for egg wash)

Cooking Directions:

Alright, folks, we're going to take a walk on the Mediterranean side with these Spinach and Feta Empanadas.

In a pan, sauté some diced onion and minced garlic until softened. Add in some chopped spinach and a 1/4 tsp of cumin powder. Give it a good stir, season it with some salt and pepper. Remove from heat and let it cool down before you start assembling your empanadas.

Next, roll out your empanada dough. I like mine to be about 1/8 inch thick. Cut out some circles. Place a tablespoon of filling on one side of the dough circle. Add some crumbled feta cheese on top. Brush the edges of the dough with the beaten egg. Fold the dough over the filling, forming a half-moon shape and press the edges to seal.

Place the empanadas on a baking sheet lined with parchment paper. Brush the top with the beaten egg. Bake those bad boys in the oven at 375F (190C) for 15-20 minutes or until golden brown. Serve 'em up nice and warm, maybe with some tzatziki or hummus on the side.

And there you have it folks, the perfect Spinach and Feta Empanadas.

Enjoy

6. Chipotle Chicken Empanadas

Prep: 15 min. Cook: 25 min. Ready in: 40 min. Servings: 4

Ingredients:

3/4 lb. shredded chicken

3/4 cup of diced chipotle pepper

1/2 onion, diced

1 1/2 cloves of garlic, minced

1/2 tsp of cumin powder

Salt and pepper to taste

3/4 package of empanada dough (store-bought or homemade)

3/4 egg, beaten (for egg wash)

Cooking Directions:

Alright folks, listen up. We're going to take a walk on the spicy side with these Chipotle chicken Empanadas. And trust me, it's a flavor explosion in your mouth.

In a pan, brown the shredded chicken over medium-high heat. Add in some diced onion, minced garlic, and a teaspoon of cumin powder. Give it a good stir and let those aromatics release their flavors. Season that with some salt and pepper, and you're on your way to flavor town. Add in some diced chipotle pepper. Remove from heat and let it cool down before you start assembling your empanadas.

Next, roll out your empanada dough. I like mine to be about 1/8 inch thick. Cut out some circles. Place a tablespoon of filling on one side of the dough circle. Brush the edges of the dough with the beaten egg. Fold the dough over the filling, forming a half-moon shape and press the edges to seal.

Place the empanadas on a baking sheet lined with parchment paper. Brush the top with the beaten egg. Bake those bad boys in the oven at 375F (190C) for 20-25 minutes or until golden brown. Serve 'em up nice and warm, maybe with some sour cream or guacamole on the side. And there you have it folks, the perfect Chipotle chicken Empanadas.

Enjoy

7. Nutella and Banana Empanadas

Prep: 15 min. Cook: 20 min. Ready in: 35 min. Servings: 4

Ingredients:

3/4 cup of Nutella spread

1 banana, mashed

1 tsp of vanilla extract

3/4 package of empanada dough (store-bought or homemade)

3/4 egg, beaten (for egg wash)

Cooking Directions:

Alright folks, listen up. We're going to take a walk on the sweet side with these Nutella and Banana Empanadas, it's a combination of flavors that just can't be beat.

In a bowl, mix Nutella, mashed banana, and vanilla extract.

Next, roll out your empanada dough. I like mine to be about 1/8 inch thick. Cut out some circles. Place a tablespoon of filling on one side of the dough circle. Brush the edges of the dough with the beaten egg. Fold the dough over the filling, forming a half-moon shape and press the edges to seal.

Place the empanadas on a baking sheet lined with parchment paper. Brush the top with the beaten egg. Bake those bad boys in the oven at 375F (190C) for 15-20 minutes or until golden brown. Serve 'em up nice and warm, maybe with some ice cream or whipped cream on the side.

And there you have it folks, the perfect Nutella, and Banana Empanadas.

Enjoy

8. BBQ Pork Empanadas

Prep: 15 min. Cook: 20 min. Ready in: 35 min. Servings: 4

Ingredients:

3/4 lb. of pulled pork

1/2 cup of BBQ sauce

1/2 onion, diced

1 clove of garlic, minced

1/4 tsp of smoked paprika

Salt and pepper to taste

3/4 package of empanada dough (store-bought or homemade)

3/4 egg, beaten (for egg wash)

Cooking Directions:

Alright folks, if you're looking for a party in your mouth, you've come to the right place. These BBQ Pork Empanadas are the perfect blend of savory and smoky flavors that will have you coming back for more. Let's get started, shall we?

In a pan, sauté some diced onion and minced garlic until softened. Add in some pulled pork, 1/4 cup of BBQ sauce, and a 1/4 tsp of smoked paprika. Give it a good stir, season it with some salt and pepper. Remove from heat and let it cool down before you start assembling your empanadas.

Next, roll out your empanada dough. I like mine to be about 1/8 inch thick. Cut out some circles. Place a tablespoon of filling on one side of the dough circle. Brush the edges of the dough with the beaten egg. Fold the dough over the filling, forming a half-moon shape and press the edges to seal.

Place the empanadas on a baking sheet lined with parchment paper. Brush the top with the beaten egg. Bake those bad boys in the oven at 375F (190C) for 15-20 minutes or until golden brown. Serve 'em up nice and warm, maybe with some coleslaw on the side.

And there you have it folks, the perfect BBQ Pork Empanadas.

Enjoy

9. Mushroom and Spinach Empanadas

Prep: 15 min. Cook: 20 min. Ready in: 35 min. Servings: 4

Ingredients:

3/4 cup of sliced mushrooms

3/4 cup of chopped spinach

1/2 onion, diced

1 clove of garlic, minced

1/4 tsp of thyme

Salt and pepper to taste

3/4 package of empanada dough (store-bought or homemade)

3/4 egg, beaten (for egg wash)

Cooking Directions:

Alright folks, if you're looking for a twist on the traditional empanada, you've come to the right place. These Mushroom and Spinach Empanadas are a delicious combination of earthy mushrooms, healthy spinach and savory spices that will elevate your empanada game. Let's get started, shall we?

In a pan, sauté some diced onion, minced garlic, and sliced mushrooms until softened. Add in some chopped spinach, a 1/4 tsp of thyme, season it with some salt and pepper. Remove from heat and let it cool down before you start assembling your empanadas.

Next, roll out your empanada dough. I like mine to be about 1/8 inch thick. Cut out some circles. Place a tablespoon of filling on one side of the dough circle. Brush the edges of the dough with the beaten egg. Fold the dough over the filling, forming a half-moon shape and press the edges to seal.

Place the empanadas on a baking sheet lined with parchment paper. Brush the top with the beaten egg. Bake those bad boys in the oven at 375F (190C) for 15-20 minutes or until golden brown. Serve 'em up nice and warm, maybe with some sour cream on the side.

And there you have it folks, the perfect Mushroom and Spinach Empanadas.

Enjoy

10. Sweet Potato and Black Bean Empanadas

Prep: 15 min. Cook: 20 min. Ready in: 35 min. Servings: 4

Ingredients:

3/4 cup of mashed sweet potatoes

3/4 cup of black beans

1/2 onion, diced

1 clove of garlic, minced

1/4 tsp of cumin

Salt and pepper to taste

3/4 package of empanada dough (store-bought or homemade)

3/4 egg, beaten (for egg wash)

Cooking Directions:

Alright folks, listen up. We're going to take a walk on the sweet side with these Sweet Potato and Black Bean Empanadas. And trust me, it's a flavor explosion in your mouth.

In a pan, sauté some diced onion and minced garlic until softened. Add in some mashed sweet potatoes, black beans, 1/4 tsp of cumin, season it with some salt and pepper. Remove from heat and let it cool down before you start assembling your empanadas.

Next, roll out your empanada dough. I like mine to be about 1/8 inch thick. Cut out some circles. Place a tablespoon of filling on one side of the dough circle. Brush the edges of the dough with the beaten egg. Fold the dough over the filling, forming a half-moon shape and press the edges to seal.

Place the empanadas on a baking sheet lined with parchment paper. Brush the top with the beaten egg. Bake those bad boys in the oven at 375F (190C) for 15-20 minutes or until golden brown. Serve 'em up nice and warm, maybe with some sour cream on the side.

And there you have it folks, the perfect Sweet Potato and Black Bean Empanadas. So go ahead, indulge in the sweet and savory flavors, but don't blame me if you can't stop at just one!

Enjoy

11. Curried Pork Empanada

Prep: 30 min. Cook: 20 min. Ready in: 50 min. Servings: 4

Ingredients:

1 pound ground pork

1/2 cup diced onion

2 tablespoons yellow curry powder

1/2 teaspoon salt

1/4 teaspoon black pepper

1 tablespoon olive oil

1 package of empanada dough

1 egg, beaten

Cooking Directions:

Ladies and gentlemen, gather around for a taste of the exotic! These Curried Pork Empanadas are a flavor extravaganza, with juicy ground pork and bold curry spices encased in a flaky, golden crust.

To start, heat the olive oil in a large skillet over medium heat. Add the onion and cook until soft and translucent, about 5 minutes. Then, add the ground pork and cook until browned, about 8-10 minutes. Stir in the curry powder, salt, and pepper, and cook for another 2-3 minutes. Set aside to cool.

Next, preheat your oven to 375°F and line a baking sheet with parchment paper. Roll out the empanada dough on a lightly floured surface to 1/8-inch thickness. Cut the dough into 4-inch rounds. Spoon about 2 tablespoons of the curried pork filling onto one half of each round, leaving a 1/2-inch border around the edges. Brush the edges with the beaten egg and fold the other half of the dough over the filling, pressing the edges to seal. Place the empanadas on the prepared baking sheet and brush the tops with the remaining egg.

Bake the empanadas for 20-25 minutes, or until they're golden brown and crispy.

And there you have it folks, the flavor adventure, the Curried Pork Empanadas. Each flaky bite is a journey to the East, with juicy ground pork and bold curry spices taking center stage. So go ahead, grab a bite, and let the good times roll!

Enjoy

12. Chicken and Cheese Empanadas

Prep: 15 min. Cook: 20 min. Ready in: 35 min. Servings: 4

Ingredients:

3/4 lb. of ground chicken

3/4 cup of diced cheese (cheddar, monterey jack, or any cheese of your choice)

1/2 onion, diced

1 clove of garlic, minced

1/4 tsp of cilantro

Salt and pepper to taste

3/4 package of empanada dough (store-bought or homemade)

3/4 egg, beaten (for egg wash)

Cooking Directions:

Folks, are you ready for a cheesy twist on the classic empanada? These Chicken and Cheese Empanadas are packed with savory chicken, gooey cheese, and a hint of cilantro for an explosion of flavor in every bite. Let's get started and get our hands dirty.

Start by browning some ground chicken in a pan, add in some diced onions and minced garlic until softened. Add in some diced cheese, 1/4 tsp of cilantro, season it with some salt and pepper. Remove from heat and let it cool down before you start assembling your empanadas. When ready, roll out your empanada dough, cut out circles and place a tablespoon of filling on one side of the dough. Brush the edges with the beaten egg, fold over, press the edges to seal. Place the empanadas on a baking sheet lined with parchment paper, brush the top with the beaten egg.

Bake in the oven at 375F (190C) for 15-20 minutes or until golden brown. Serve 'em up nice and warm, maybe with some sour cream on the side.

And there you have it folks, the perfect Chicken and Cheese Empanadas. So go ahead, indulge in the cheesy and savory flavors, and enjoy the taste of these delicious treats. Embrace the cheesy goodness and get ready to fall in love

Enjoy

13. Shrimp and Mango Empanadas

Prep: 40 min. Cook: 20 min. Ready in: 60 min. Servings: 12

Ingredients:

3/4 lb. of cooked shrimp, peeled and diced

3/4 cup of diced mango

1/2 onion, diced

1 clove of garlic, minced

1/4 tsp of cumin

Salt and pepper to taste

3/4 package of empanada dough (store-bought or homemade)

3/4 egg, beaten (for egg wash)

Cooking Directions:

Alright folks, listen up. We're going to take a walk on the sweet and savory side with these Shrimp and Mango Empanadas. And trust me, it's a flavor explosion in your mouth.

In a pan, sauté some diced onion and minced garlic until softened. Add in some diced cooked shrimp, diced mango, 1/4 tsp of cumin, season it with some salt and pepper. Remove from heat and let it cool down before you start assembling your empanadas.

Next, roll out your empanada dough. I like mine to be about 1/8 inch thick. Cut out some circles. Place a tablespoon of filling on one side of the dough circle. Brush the edges of the dough with the beaten egg. Fold the dough over the filling, forming a half-moon shape and press the edges to seal.

Place the empanadas on a baking sheet lined with parchment paper. Brush the top with the beaten egg. Bake those bad boys in the oven at 375F (190C) for 15-20 minutes or until golden brown. Serve 'em up nice and warm, maybe with some sour cream on the side.

And there you have it folks, the perfect Shrimp and Mango Empanadas. So go ahead, indulge in the sweet and savory flavors, and enjoy the taste of these delicious treats. Embrace the sweet and savory combination and get ready to fall in love. Embrace the tropical flavors and enjoy the perfect balance of sweet and savory.

Enjoy

14. Pork and Apple Empanadas

Prep: 15 min. Cook: 20 min. Ready in: 35 min. Servings: 4

Ingredients:

1 lb. ground pork

1 granny smith apple, peeled and diced

1/2 onion, diced

1/4 cup raisins

1/4 cup chopped cilantro

1 tsp cumin

1/2 tsp smoked paprika

1/4 tsp salt

1/4 tsp pepper

1 package of empanada wrappers (8-12 wrappers)

1 egg, beaten for egg wash

oil for frying

Cooking Directions:

Alright, let's get our hands dirty and make some bloody delicious Pork and Apple Empanadas. This recipe will serve 4 people, so let's make sure we have enough ingredients.

First, we're going to start by browning the ground pork in a pan over medium heat. Once it's cooked through, add in the diced onion and apple. Cook for a few minutes until the onion is translucent. Next, add in the raisins, cilantro, cumin, smoked paprika, salt, and pepper. Give it a good stir and let it cook for another 5 minutes. Remove from heat and let it cool.

While the pork mixture cools, take your empanada wrappers, and place a spoonful of the mixture on one half of the wrapper. Brush the edges with the beaten egg and fold the wrapper in half to create a half-moon shape. Press the edges to seal the empanada. Repeat this process until you have used up all the pork mixture.

Now, in a deep pan or a fryer, heat up some oil to 350 degrees F. Carefully add the empanadas and fry them for about 2-3 minutes on each side, or until golden brown.

Remove from the oil and let them cool for a few minutes. These Pork and Apple Empanadas are bloody perfect as a snack or an appetizer, but you can also serve them with a nice green salad for a complete meal. Enjoy, you bloody legends!

Enjoy

15. Black Bean and Cheese Empanadas

Prep: 15 min. Cook: 20 min. Ready in: 35 min. Servings: 4

Ingredients:

1 can black beans, drained and rinsed

1/2 onion, diced

1/4 cup diced red bell pepper

1/4 cup chopped cilantro

1/4 cup diced jalapeño pepper (optional)

1 tsp cumin

1/2 tsp smoked paprika

1/4 tsp salt

1/4 tsp pepper

1 cup shredded cheddar cheese

1 package of empanada wrappers

1 egg, beaten for egg wash

oil for frying

Cooking Directions:

Get ready for some serious flavor explosion, as we're about to make some Black Bean and Cheese Empanadas that are going to knock your socks off. We'll be using a combination of black beans, onions, red bell pepper, cilantro, and spices, that will be perfectly balanced with the addition of melted cheese, all wrapped in a crispy and flaky pastry. So, preheat your fryer or a deep pan and let's begin this culinary journey.

First, we're going to start by sautéing the diced onion and red bell pepper in a pan over medium heat. Once it's cooked through, add in the black beans, cilantro, jalapeño pepper (if using), cumin, smoked paprika, salt, and pepper. Give it a good stir and let it cook for another 5 minutes. Remove from heat and let it cool.

While the black bean mixture cools, take your empanada wrappers and place a spoonful of the mixture on one half of the wrapper. Then add a good pinch of shredded cheese, Brush the edges with the beaten egg and fold the wrapper in half to create a half-moon shape. Press the edges to seal the empanada. Repeat this process until you have used up all the black bean mixture.

Now, in a deep pan or a fryer, heat up some oil to 350 degrees F. Carefully add the empanadas and fry them for about 2-3 minutes on each side, or until golden brown.

Remove from the oil and let them cool for a few minutes. These Black Bean and Cheese Empanadas are bloody perfect as a snack or an appetizer, but you can also serve them with a nice green salad for a complete meal. Enjoy, you bloody legends!

Enjoy

16. Salmon and Dill Empanadas

Prep: 15 min. Cook: 20 min. Ready in: 35 min. Servings: 4

Ingredients:

1 lb. cooked salmon, flaked

1/2 onion, diced

1/4 cup chopped dill

1/4 cup sour cream

1/4 tsp salt

1/4 tsp pepper

1 package of empanada wrappers

1 egg, beaten for egg wash

oil for frying

Cooking Directions:

Listen, I've been around the world, and I've eaten some of the most exotic and interesting dishes, but I gotta tell you, these Salmon and Dill Empanadas are something special.

First, in a mixing bowl, we're going to combine the flaked salmon, diced onion, chopped dill, sour cream, salt, and pepper. Give it a good mix, you should smell the freshness of the dill and the richness of the salmon. Now, take your empanada wrappers and place a spoonful of the salmon mixture on one half of the wrapper. Brush the edges with the beaten egg and fold the wrapper in half to create a half-moon shape. Press the edges to seal the empanada. Repeat this process until you have used up all the salmon mixture. Now, we're going to deep fry these bad boys, so in a deep pan or a fryer, heat up some oil to 350 degrees F. Carefully add the empanadas and fry them for about 2-3 minutes on each side, or until golden brown. Trust me, the smell of the frying empanadas will make your mouth water. Once they're golden brown and crispy, remove them from the oil and let them cool for a few minutes. These Salmon and Dill Empanadas are the perfect combination of flavors, the richness of the salmon, the freshness of the dill, and the creaminess of the sour cream. Serve them as a snack or an appetizer, but you can also serve them with a nice green salad for a complete meal.

But let me tell you, these empanadas are so good, you might not want to share them. But hey, that's the beauty of food, it's meant to be shared and enjoyed with the people you love. So, go ahead, make these empanadas, and enjoy them while they're hot and crispy, they're truly a delight.

Enjoy

17. Mushroom and Goat Cheese Empanadas

Prep: 35 min. Cook: 25 min. Ready in: 50 min. Servings: 4

Ingredients:

8 oz mushrooms, sliced

1/2 onion, diced

1/4 cup chopped parsley

1/4 cup crumbled goat cheese

1/4 tsp salt

1/4 tsp pepper

1 package of empanada wrappers

1 egg, beaten for egg wash

oil for frying

Cooking Directions:

Alright, folks, gather around, we're going to make some empanadas that will make your taste buds sing.

First, in a pan over medium heat, sauté the mushrooms and diced onion until the mushrooms are tender and the onion is translucent. Remove from heat and let it cool. Once it's cool, in a mixing bowl, we're going to combine the mushroom mixture, chopped parsley, crumbled goat cheese, salt, and pepper. Give it a good mix, you should smell the earthiness of the mushrooms and the tanginess of the goat cheese.

Now, take your empanada wrappers and place a spoonful of the mushroom mixture on one half of the wrapper. Brush the edges with the beaten egg and fold the wrapper in half to create a half-moon shape. Press the edges to seal the empanada. Repeat this process until you have used up all the mushroom mixture.

Now, we're going to deep fry these bad boys, so in a deep pan or a fryer, heat up some oil to 350 degrees F. Carefully add the empanadas and fry them for about 2-3 minutes on each side, or until golden brown. Trust me, the smell of the frying empanadas will make your mouth water. Once they're golden brown and crispy, remove them from the oil and let them cool for a few minutes. These Mushroom and Goat Cheese Empanadas are the perfect combination of flavors, the earthiness of the mushrooms, the tanginess of the goat cheese, and the freshness of the parsley. Serve them as a snack or an appetizer, but you can also serve them with a nice green salad for a complete meal.

Enjoy

18. Shrimp and Scallop Empanadas

Prep: 15 min. Cook: 20 min. Ready in: 35 min. Servings: 4

Ingredients:

8 oz cooked shrimp, chopped

8 oz cooked scallops, chopped

1/2 onion, diced

1/4 cup chopped cilantro

1/4 cup diced red pepper

1/4 tsp salt

1/4 tsp cumin

1/4 tsp smoked paprika

1 package of empanada wrappers

1 egg, beaten for egg wash

oil for frying

Cooking Directions:

Alright, folks, gather around, we're going to make some empanadas that will make you want to pack your bags and travel the world.

First, we're going to take the shrimp and scallops, the jewels of the sea and chop them up. In a pan over medium heat, sauté the shrimp and scallops with diced onion, cilantro, red pepper, salt, cumin, and a pinch of smoked paprika until everything is well combined and heated through. Remove from heat and let it cool.

Now, take your empanada wrappers and place a spoonful of the seafood mixture on one half of the wrapper. Brush the edges with the beaten egg and fold the wrapper in half to create a half-moon shape. Press the edges to seal the empanada. Repeat this process until you have used up all the seafood mixture.

Now, we're going to deep fry these bad boys, so in a deep pan or a fryer, heat up some oil to 350 degrees F. Carefully add the empanadas and fry them for about 2-3 minutes on each side, or until golden brown. Trust me, the smell of the frying empanadas will make your mouth water and transport you to a beachside shack in the Caribbean.

Enjoy

19. Tuna and Olive Empanada

Prep: 30 min. Cook: 30 min. Ready in: 60 min. Servings: 4

Ingredients:

1 cup all-purpose flour

1/2 teaspoon salt

1/4 cup cold butter, diced

1/4 cup cold shortening, diced

1/4 cup ice water

1 can (7 ounces) tuna, drained

1/4 cup chopped green olives

1/4 cup chopped pimiento-stuffed olives

1/4 cup chopped onion

1 egg yolk, lightly beaten

Cooking Directions:

Alright folks, listen up. This recipe for Tuna and Olive Empanadas is a classic, it's simple and it's delicious. It's going to take you about 30 minutes to prep, and another 30 minutes to cook. But trust me, it's worth the wait.

First things first, let's make the dough. In a large mixing bowl, combine the flour and salt. Cut in the butter and shortening until the mixture resembles coarse crumbs. Gradually add the ice water, stirring with a fork until the dough forms a ball. Cover and refrigerate for 30 minutes. Now, while that's chillin', let's get the filling together. In a medium mixing bowl, combine the tuna, olives, onion, and pimiento. Mix well. When the dough is chilled, roll it out into a large circle on a lightly floured surface. Using a round cutter or a glass, cut the dough into 4-inch circles.

Now, this is the fun part. Take one of the circles and spoon a heaping tablespoon of the tuna mixture onto one half of the circle. Brush the edge with the egg yolk, then fold the dough over and press the edges together to seal. Repeat with the remaining dough and filling.

Place the empanadas on a baking sheet and brush them with the remaining egg yolk. Pop them in a preheated 350 degrees F oven for about 30 minutes, or until golden brown.

Serve them hot and enjoy, folks. These empanadas are the perfect combination of salty and savory. They're a classic dish that everyone should try at least once in their life.

Enjoy

20. Egg and Cheese Empanadas

Prep: 20 min. Cook: 30 min. Ready in: 50 min. Servings: 4

Ingredients:

1 package of store-bought empanada dough

4 eggs

1 cup of shredded cheese

Salt and pepper, to taste

1 egg, beaten (for egg wash)

Cooking Directions:

Listen up folks, I got a recipe for you that's going to knock your socks off. These Egg and Cheese Empanadas are the real deal. I'm talking flaky, golden-brown dough with a warm, gooey center of scrambled eggs and melted cheese. And the best part? You can make them in under an hour, using store-bought dough. So, forget about the fancy, fancy. Let's get down and dirty with some empanadas.

First things first, preheat that oven to 375 degrees. Trust me, you don't want to skimp on the heat. Next, scramble some eggs in a skillet, seasoning with salt and pepper to taste. Once they're cooked, let them cool.

Now, take that store-bought dough and roll it out on a floured surface. Cut out circles with a round cutter. Place a spoonful of scrambled eggs and a sprinkle of shredded cheese in the center of each dough circle. Fold the dough over to form a half-moon shape and press the edges to seal. Brush the top of each empanada with beaten egg.

Place the empanadas on a baking sheet and pop them in the oven for 20 minutes, or until golden brown. And there you have it, folks. The perfect snack or meal, ready in under an hour. Serve them up with a cold beer and enjoy the goodness.

Enjoy

21. Turkey and Cranberry Empanadas

Prep: 30 min. Cook: 20 min. Ready in: 50 min. Servings: 4

Ingredients:

1 package of store-bought empanada dough

1 cup of cooked turkey, diced

1/4 cup of cranberry sauce

1/4 cup of chopped scallions

1/4 cup of shredded cheese

Salt and pepper, to taste

1 egg, beaten (for egg wash)

Cooking Directions:

Listen up folks, I got a recipe for you that's going to change the game. These Turkey and Cranberry Empanadas are a perfect way to use up that leftover turkey from Thanksgiving. I'm talking tender, juicy turkey combined with tangy cranberry sauce, and a hint of scallions and cheese, all wrapped up in a flaky, golden-brown crust.

First things first, preheat that oven to 375 degrees. Trust me, you don't want to skimp on the heat. Next, take that cooked turkey and dice it up, throw it in a mixing bowl with cranberry sauce, scallions, cheese, and season with salt and pepper to taste.

Now, take that store-bought dough and roll it out on a floured surface. Cut out circles with a round cutter. Place a spoonful of the turkey mixture in the center of each dough circle. Fold the dough over to form a half-moon shape and press the edges to seal. Brush the top of each empanada with beaten egg.

Place the empanadas on a baking sheet and pop them in the oven for 20 minutes, or until golden brown. Serve them up with a cold beer and enjoy the goodness.

And trust me, these empanadas will be a hit at any party or gathering. So, don't be afraid to experiment and try out different fillings, the possibilities are endless. Embrace the empanadas.

Enjoy

22. Beef and Mushroom Empanadas

Prep: 15 min. Cook: 20 min. Ready in: 35 min. Servings: 8

Ingredients:

1 lb. ground beef

1/2 onion, diced

1/2 cup diced mushrooms

1/4 cup chopped fresh parsley

1/4 cup raisins

1/4 cup chopped green olives

1/4 cup diced green bell pepper

2 cloves garlic, minced

2 tablespoons tomato paste

1 teaspoon ground cumin

1/2 teaspoon salt

1/4 teaspoon black pepper

2 tablespoons olive oil

1 egg, beaten

store-bought empanada dough

Cooking Directions:

Listen, folks, you wanna make some empanadas that'll knock the socks off your friends and family? You gotta start with the filling, and let me tell you, this beef and mushroom mixture is a real winner.

First, heat a large skillet over medium-high heat and add the olive oil. Once that oil is hot, toss in the onions, garlic, bell pepper and mushrooms. Cook until softened, about 5 minutes. Add the ground beef, cumin, salt, and pepper. Cook until the beef is browned, about 5-7 minutes. Now, you're going to add in the raisins, olives, parsley, and tomato paste. Cook for another 2-3 minutes, stirring frequently. You want all those flavors to meld together, to create a filling that's going to make your taste buds dance. Once that filling is done, take it off the heat and let it cool. This is important, because if you try to put hot filling in your empanadas, it's going to make a mess of your dough. Trust me, I've made that mistake before. Now, preheat your oven to 375F.

Take your store-bought empanada dough, roll it out, and cut it into circles. Place a spoonful of the beef and mushroom mixture in the center of each circle. Brush the edges with the beaten egg, and then fold the dough over, pressing the edges to seal.

Place the empanadas on a baking sheet and brush the tops with the remaining beaten egg. Bake for 20 minutes or until golden brown.

And there you have it folks, Beef and Mushroom Empanadas that are going to make you the star of the show. Pair it with a cold beer and enjoy the ride, you deserve it.

Enjoy

23. Chicken and Spinach Empanadas

Prep: 20 min. Cook: 20 min. Ready in: 40 min. Servings: 4

Ingredients:

1 lb. boneless, skinless chicken breasts, diced

1 onion, diced

3 cloves of garlic, minced

1 cup of frozen spinach, thawed and drained

1/4 cup of cilantro, chopped

1/4 cup of parsley, chopped

1/4 cup of diced green olives

2 tablespoons of olive oil

1 teaspoon of ground cumin

1/2 teaspoon of ground paprika

Salt and pepper, to taste

1 package of store-bought empanada dough

1 egg, beaten (for egg wash)

Cooking Directions:

Alright folks, listen up. I'm going to show you how to make some damn good empanadas.

First thing you're going to do is heat up 2 tablespoons of olive oil in a pan over medium-high heat. Once that oil is hot, toss in your diced chicken and cook it until it's nice and browned. While that's happening, finely dice up a medium onion and mince 3 cloves of garlic. Once the chicken is cooked, toss in the onions and garlic, and cook for a couple of minutes until they're softened. Next up, add in 1 cup of thawed and drained spinach, 1/4 cup of chopped cilantro, 1/4 cup of chopped parsley, 1/4 cup of diced green olives, 1 teaspoon of ground cumin, and 1/2 teaspoon of ground paprika. Cook that mixture for another 2-3 minutes until everything is well combined. Season with salt and pepper to taste. Now, it's time to assemble the empanadas. Preheat your oven to 375 degrees F. Roll out the store-bought empanada dough and cut it into circles. Place a heaping spoonful of the chicken and spinach filling onto one half of each dough circle. Brush the edges with beaten egg and fold the other half of the dough over the filling to create a half-moon shape. Press the edges together to seal the empanada. Once all your empanadas are assembled, brush them with a little bit of the beaten egg and place them on a baking sheet. Bake them in the preheated oven for 20 minutes or until they're golden brown and crispy.

And there you have it, folks. A delicious and easy recipe for Chicken and Spinach Empanadas that will knock the socks off your dinner guests. Don't be afraid to experiment with different fillings, and always remember good food is all about taking risks. And these empanadas are a risk worth taking.

Enjoy

24. Pork and Pineapple Empanadas

Prep: 30 min. Cook: 2 h Ready in: 2 h 30 min. Servings: 4

Ingredients:

1 pound pork shoulder, diced
1/2 cup diced pineapple
1/4 cup diced red onion
1/4 cup diced red bell pepper
1/4 cup diced green bell pepper
1/4 cup diced yellow bell pepper
1/4 cup diced jalapeño pepper
1/4 cup diced cilantro
1/4 cup diced green onion
1/4 cup diced garlic
1/4 cup diced ginger
1/4 cup diced tomato
1/4 cup diced chicken stock
1/4 cup diced nutmeg
1/4 cup diced allspice
1/4 cup diced cloves
1/4 cup diced bay leaves
1/4 cup diced thyme
1/4 cup diced oregano
1/4 cup diced marjoram

1/4 cup diced pineapple juice
1/4 cup diced soy sauce
1/4 cup diced sake
1/4 cup diced olive oil
1/4 cup diced cornstarch
1/4 cup diced water
1/4 cup diced sugar
1/4 cup diced salt
1/4 cup diced black pepper
1/4 cup diced cumin
1/4 cup diced paprika
1/4 cup diced chili powder
1/4 cup diced cayenne pepper
1/4 cup diced cinnamon

1/4 cup diced rosemary
1/4 cup diced basil
1/4 cup diced parsley
1/4 cup diced cilantro
1/4 cup diced green onion
1 package of store-bought empanada dough

Cooking Directions:

Listen up, kids, this one's a little bit of a project, but trust me when I say it's worth it. These Pork and Pineapple Empanadas are going to knock your socks off.

First thing's first, let's get our pork diced up nice and small. We're going to give it a little bath in a marinade made of pineapple juice, soy sauce, sake, olive oil, and all those spices I listed off earlier. Let that sit in the fridge for at least an hour, but overnight is even better.

While the pork's marinating, we're going to start prepping our filling. Take a look at that list of vegetables I gave you, we're going to dice all that up nice and small. Once that's done, we're going to sauté it all in a pan with a little bit of oil, and then mix it in with our pork. We're going to let that simmer on low heat for about an hour and a half, or until the pork is nice and tender.

Once the filling is done, we're going to roll out our store-bought empanada dough, and start filling and folding those bad boys. Make sure to crimp the edges nice and tight so none of that filling falls out.

Pop those empanadas in the oven at 350 degrees for about 15-20 minutes, or until the dough is nice and golden brown. And just like that, you've got yourself some damn fine Pork and Pineapple Empanadas. Serve it up with a cold beer and enjoy!

Enjoy

25. Black Bean and Sweet Potato Empanadas

55

Prep: 30 min. Cook: 15 min. Ready in: 45 min. Servings: 4

Ingredients:

1 can of black beans, drained and rinsed

1 medium sweet potato, peeled and diced

1/2 red onion, diced

1 jalapeño pepper, diced

2 cloves of garlic, minced

1 teaspoon ground cumin

1/2 teaspoon chili powder

Salt and pepper, to taste

1/4 cup cilantro, chopped

1 store-bought empanada dough

1 egg, beaten (for brushing the empanadas)

Cooking Directions:

Listen folks, these empanadas are the real deal.

We're going to start by prepping our filling. Take that sweet potato, peel it, and dice it up nice and small. That's going to give us some sweetness to balance out the heat from the jalapeño.

Next, we're going to add some diced red onion and minced garlic. These are going to give us some depth of flavor and make sure these empanadas aren't one note.

Now, we're going to add our black beans, cumin, chili powder, and a pinch of salt and pepper. Make sure everything is well combined.

Now, we're going to roll out our store-bought dough, and spoon a generous amount of our filling onto each empanada. Make sure you don't overstuff them, or they'll burst open in the oven.

Fold the dough over the filling and press the edges to seal them shut. Now, take that beaten egg and brush it over the top of each empanada. Pop them in the oven for 20 minutes, or until they're golden brown and crispy.

And voila! You've got yourself some Black Bean and Sweet Potato Empanadas that'll knock your socks off. Serve it with some cilantro and sour cream, and you're in for a treat.

Enjoy

26. Oven Baked Beef Empanadas

Prep: 30 min. Cook: 20 min. Ready in: 50 min. Servings: 4

Ingredients:

1 lb. salmon fillet, skin removed and cut into small cubes

1 bunch asparagus, trimmed and cut into small pieces

1 small onion, finely chopped

1 garlic clove, minced

1 tbsp olive oil

1/2 tsp cumin

1/4 tsp smoked paprika

1/4 tsp salt

1/4 tsp black pepper

1 cup shredded cheddar cheese

1 store-bought empanada dough

1 egg, beaten

Cooking Directions:

Listen up folks, it's time to elevate your empanada game.

We're going to start by prepping our fillings. Take that beautiful piece of salmon and chop it up into small cubes. Make sure to get rid of any skin, we don't need that in our empanadas. Next, take those fresh asparagus stalks and chop them up into small pieces.

In a pan, heat up some olive oil and add in the onions and garlic. Cook until the onions are translucent. Now, throw in the cumin, smoked paprika, salt, and pepper, and give it a good stir. Add in the salmon and asparagus and cook until the salmon is cooked through, and the asparagus is tender.

Take that mixture off the heat and let it cool for a bit. While that's cooling, take your store-bought dough and roll it out to about 1/8-inch thickness. Cut out circles from the dough, you should get about 8 circles. Place a spoonful of the salmon and asparagus mixture in the center of each dough circle. Top it off with a sprinkle of shredded cheddar cheese.

Now, take your beaten egg and brush the edges of each dough circle. Fold the dough in half and press the edges to seal the empanadas. Use a fork to press the edges together.

Brush the top of each empanada with the remaining beaten egg. Place the empanadas on a baking sheet lined with parchment paper and bake them in a preheated oven at 375F for 20 minutes or until the empanadas are golden brown and crispy.

Ladies and gentlemen, your Salmon and Asparagus Empanadas are ready to be devoured. These babies are the perfect balance of savory and crispy, a perfect little package of flavor. Don't be afraid to experiment with different fillings, the possibilities are endless.

Enjoy

27. Shrimp and Mushroom Empanadas

Prep: 20 min. Cook: 30 min. Ready in: 50 min. Servings: 4

Ingredients:

1 lb. shrimp, peeled and deveined

1/2 lb. mushrooms, sliced

1/2 small onion, diced

3 cloves garlic, minced

1/4 cup chopped cilantro

1/2 teaspoon smoked paprika

1/4 teaspoon cayenne pepper

1/2 teaspoon salt

1/4 teaspoon black pepper

1 egg, beaten

1 package of store-bought empanada dough

Cooking Directions:

Listen up folks, this recipe for Shrimp and Mushroom Empanadas is about to elevate your game. I'm talking crispy, flaky dough with a filling that's packed with flavor. It's a party in your mouth, and you're the host.

First things first, let's get the filling going. Heat a large skillet over medium-high heat and add a little bit of oil. Once that's hot, toss in your shrimp. Cook them for about 2 minutes on each side, or until they're pink and cooked through. Remove them from the skillet and set them aside.

Next up, the mushrooms. Throw 'em in the skillet and cook them until they're nice and brown. Add the onions and garlic, and cook for another 2 minutes, or until they're soft. Stir in the cilantro, smoked paprika, cayenne pepper, salt, and black pepper.

Now, it's time to bring it all together. Chop up the cooked shrimp and add it to the mushroom mixture. Mix everything together until it's well combined.

Time to roll out your dough. Dust your work surface with a little bit of flour and roll out the dough to about 1/8-inch thickness. Cut out circles of dough, about 4 inches in diameter.

Brush the edges of the dough circles with the beaten egg. Place a heaping tablespoon of the shrimp and mushroom mixture in the center of each circle. Fold the dough over and press the edges together to seal. Brush the top of each empanada with more beaten egg.

Pop 'em in the oven at 375 degrees F for 20 minutes, or until they're golden brown and crispy. And that, my friends, is how you make empanadas that'll make your taste buds sing.

Serve them up with a cold beer!

Enjoy

28. Tuna and Green Olive Empanadas

Prep: 20 min. Cook: 20 min. Ready in: 40 min. Servings: 4

Ingredients:

1 can of tuna in oil, drained

1/4 cup of chopped green olives

1/4 cup of diced onion

2 cloves of garlic, minced

1/4 cup of chopped fresh cilantro

Salt and pepper, to taste

1 package of store-bought empanada dough

1 egg, beaten, for egg wash

Cooking Directions:

Alright folks, gather round, I got a recipe that's going to knock your socks off. Tuna and Green Olive Empanadas, the perfect blend of savory and tangy. And the best part is they're easy to make, so you can impress your guests without breaking a sweat. Let's get started.

First things first, preheat that oven to 375F (190C). While that's heating up, let's get the filling ready. In a medium bowl, mix the tuna, green olives, onion, garlic, cilantro, salt, and pepper. Now, this is going to be the heart and soul of our empanadas. A good filling is the key to a good empanada. Roll out the empanada dough on a lightly floured surface. Alright, now we got our dough, it's store-bought so it's going to be easy. Roll it out nice and thin, we don't want it too thick.
Use a round cookie cutter or a glass to cut out 4-inch circles. Now you got your circles, make sure they're nice and round, unless you're into that rustic look. Place a heaping tablespoon of the tuna mixture on one half of each dough circle. Now, this is where the magic happens, spoon a nice amount of the filling on one half of the circle, not too much, not too little. Leave a little bit of space around the edges. Brush the edges of the dough with the beaten egg and fold the dough over, pressing the edges together to seal. Fold it over, press the edges together, you want to make sure it's sealed good, otherwise, the filling's going to fall out. Brush the tops of the empanadas with the remaining beaten egg and make a few small slits on the top of each empanada. Brush the top with the egg wash, it's going to give it that nice golden color. And don't forget the slits, it's going to let the steam out. Place the empanadas on a baking sheet lined with parchment paper and bake for 20-25 minutes, or until golden brown. In the oven they go, 20-25 minutes and you got yourself a masterpiece. Remove from the oven and let them cool for a few minutes before serving. Take them out of the oven, let them cool for a bit, you don't want to burn your mouth, trust me.
And there you have it folks, Tuna and Green Olive Empanadas that are as delicious as they are easy to make. I guarantee they'll be a hit at your next dinner party or game night. So go ahead, impress your friends and family with your culinary skills.

<u>Enjoy</u>

29. Egg and Chorizo Empanadas

Prep: 20 min. Cook: 20 min. Ready in: 40 min. Servings: 4

Ingredients:

1/2-pound Mexican chorizo, casings removed

1/2 cup diced onion

1/2 cup diced red bell pepper

1/4 cup diced jalapeno pepper

1/4 cup diced poblano pepper

1/4 cup diced green bell pepper

1/2 teaspoon ground cumin

1/2 teaspoon smoked paprika

1/4 teaspoon cayenne pepper

1/4 teaspoon black pepper

1/4 teaspoon salt

4 large eggs

1/4 cup heavy cream

1/4 cup grated cheddar cheese

1/4 cup grated Monterey Jack cheese

1/4 cup grated queso fresco

1 package (15 oz) store-bought empanada dough

1 large egg, beaten with 1 tablespoon water

Cooking Directions:

Alright, listen up folks, this recipe for Egg and Chorizo Empanadas is a game changer.

First things first, preheat your oven to 375 degrees F. Next, heat a skillet over medium-high heat and cook the chorizo until browned, about 5 minutes. Remove the chorizo from the skillet with a slotted spoon and set it aside. Add the onion, red bell pepper, jalapeno pepper, poblano pepper, and green bell pepper to the skillet, and cook until softened, about 5 minutes. Stir in the cumin, smoked paprika, cayenne pepper, black pepper, and salt. Cook for another minute. In a separate bowl, whisk together the eggs and heavy cream. Pour the mixture into the skillet and cook, stirring constantly, until the eggs are set, about 5 minutes. Stir in the chorizo, cheddar cheese, Monterey Jack cheese, and queso fresco. Now it's time to assemble the empanadas. Roll out the empanada dough on a lightly floured surface to about 1/8-inch thickness. Cut the dough into 4-inch circles using a round cookie cutter or the rim of a glass. Spoon about 2 tablespoons of the chorizo and egg filling onto one half of each dough circle, leaving a 1/2-inch border around the edges. Brush the beaten egg around the edges of the dough, then fold the dough over the filling to form a half-moon shape. Press the edges together to seal.

Place the empanadas on a baking sheet and brush the tops with the remaining beaten egg. Bake for 20 minutes, or until golden brown.

Serve hot, garnished with fresh chopped cilantro, or with a spicy salsa on the side. And don't forget a cold beer because these empanadas are going to knock your socks off.

Enjoy

30. Beef and Blue Cheese Empanadas

Prep: 20 min. Cook: 20 min. Ready In: 40 min. Servings: 4

Ingredients:

1 pound ground beef

1/2 cup diced onion

1/2 cup diced red bell pepper

1/4 cup diced jalapeno pepper

1/4 cup diced poblano pepper

1/4 cup diced green bell pepper

1/2 teaspoon ground cumin

1/2 teaspoon smoked paprika

1/4 teaspoon cayenne pepper

1/4 teaspoon black pepper

1/4 teaspoon salt

1/4 cup crumbled blue cheese

1/4 cup grated cheddar cheese

1/4 cup grated Monterey Jack cheese

1 package (15 oz) store-bought empanada dough

1 large egg, beaten with 1 tablespoon water

Cooking Directions:

Get ready for a flavorful explosion with these Beef and Blue Cheese Empanadas. The perfect combination of savory beef and tangy blue cheese in a flaky crust. Let's get cooking!

First things first, preheat your oven to 375 degrees F. Next, heat a skillet over medium-high heat and cook the beef until browned, about 5 minutes. Remove the beef from the skillet with a slotted spoon and set it aside. Add the onion, red bell pepper, jalapeno pepper, poblano pepper, and green bell pepper to the skillet, and cook until softened, about 5 minutes. Stir in the cumin, smoked paprika, cayenne pepper, black pepper, and salt. Cook for another minute. Stir in the crumbled blue cheese, cheddar cheese and Monterey Jack cheese into the beef mixture, cook until cheese melted. Now it's time to assemble the empanadas. Roll out the empanada dough on a lightly floured surface to about 1/8-inch thickness. Cut the dough into 4-inch circles using a round cookie cutter or the rim of a glass. Spoon about 2 tablespoons of the beef and blue cheese filling onto one half of each dough circle, leaving a 1/2-inch border around the edges. Brush the beaten egg around the edges of the dough, then fold the dough over the filling to form a half-moon shape. Press the edges together to seal. Place the empanadas on a baking sheet and brush the tops with the remaining beaten egg. Bake for 20 minutes, or until golden brown. Serve hot, garnished with fresh chopped parsley, or with a spicy salsa on the side. And don't forget a cold beer because these empanadas are going to be a hit.

Enjoy

31. Chicken and Broccoli Empanadas

Prep: 20 min. Cook: 20 min. Ready In: 40 min. Servings: 4

Ingredients:

1-pound boneless, skinless chicken breasts, diced

1/2 cup diced onion

1/2 cup diced red bell pepper

1/4 cup diced jalapeno pepper

1 cup chopped broccoli florets

1/4 teaspoon cayenne pepper

1/4 teaspoon black pepper

1/4 teaspoon salt

1/4 cup grated cheddar cheese

1/4 cup grated Monterey Jack cheese

1 package (15 oz) store-bought empanada dough

1 large egg, beaten with 1 tablespoon water

Cooking Directions:

Alright folks, get ready for a treat, these Chicken and Broccoli Empanadas are going to be a hit.

First things first, preheat your oven to 375 degrees F. Next, heat a skillet over medium-high heat and cook the chicken until browned, about 5 minutes. Remove the chicken from the skillet with a slotted spoon and set it aside. Add the onion, red bell pepper, jalapeno pepper and broccoli to the skillet, and cook until softened, about 5 minutes. Stir in the cayenne pepper, black pepper, and salt. Cook for another minute. Stir in the chicken, cheddar cheese and Monterey Jack cheese into the skillet, cook until cheese melted.

Now it's time to assemble the empanadas. Roll out the empanada dough on a lightly floured surface to about 1/8-inch thickness. Cut the dough into 4-inch circles using a round cookie cutter or the rim of a glass. Spoon about 2 tablespoons of the chicken and broccoli filling onto one half of each dough circle, leaving a 1/2-inch border around the edges. Brush the beaten egg around the edges of the dough, then fold the dough over the filling to form a half-moon shape. Press the edges together to seal.

Place the empanadas on a baking sheet and brush the tops with the remaining beaten egg. Bake for 20 minutes, or until golden brown.

Serve hot, garnished with fresh chopped parsley, or with a spicy salsa on the side. And don't forget a cold beer because these empanadas are going to be a hit.

Enjoy

32. Beef and Onion Empanadas

Prep: 20 min. Cook: 20 min. Ready In: 40 min. Servings: 4

Ingredients:

1 pound ground beef

1/2 cup diced onion

1/4 teaspoon cumin

1/4 teaspoon smoked paprika

1/4 teaspoon black pepper

1/4 teaspoon salt

1/4 cup grated cheddar cheese

1/4 cup grated Monterey Jack cheese

1 package (15 oz) store-bought empanada dough

1 large egg, beaten with 1 tablespoon water

Cooking Directions:

Alright folks, get ready for a delicious treat with these Beef and Onion Empanadas.

First things first, preheat your oven to 375 degrees F. Next, heat a skillet over medium-high heat and cook the beef until browned, about 5 minutes. Remove the beef from the skillet with a slotted spoon and set it aside. Add the diced onion to the skillet, and cook until softened, about 5 minutes. Stir in the cumin, smoked paprika, black pepper, and salt. Cook for another minute. Stir in the beef, cheddar cheese and Monterey Jack cheese into the skillet, cook until cheese melted.

Now it's time to assemble the empanadas. Roll out the empanada dough on a lightly floured surface to about 1/8-inch thickness. Cut the dough into 4-inch circles using a round cookie cutter or the rim of a glass.

Spoon about 2 tablespoons of the beef and onion filling onto one half of each dough circle, leaving a 1/2-inch border around the edges. Brush the beaten egg around the edges of the dough, then fold the dough over the filling to form a half-moon shape. Press the edges together to seal. Place the empanadas on a baking sheet and brush the tops with the remaining beaten egg. Bake for 20 minutes, or until golden brown.

Serve hot, garnished with fresh chopped parsley, or with a spicy salsa on the side. And don't forget a cold beer because these empanadas are going to be a hit.

Enjoy

33. Black Bean and Corn Empanadas

Prep: 20 min. Cook: 20 min. Ready In: 40 min. Servings: 4

Ingredients:

1 can black beans, drained and rinsed

1/2 cup frozen corn

1/4 cup diced onion

1/4 cup diced red bell pepper

1/4 teaspoon cumin

1/4 teaspoon smoked paprika

1/4 teaspoon black pepper

1/4 teaspoon salt

1/4 cup grated cheddar cheese

1/4 cup grated Monterey Jack cheese

1 package (15 oz) store-bought empanada dough

1 large egg, beaten with 1 tablespoon water

Cooking Directions:

Alright folks, if you're looking for a delicious and hearty empanada recipe that's a little out of the ordinary, then look no further than these Black Bean and Corn Empanadas.

First, we're going to preheat that oven to 375 degrees F. In a skillet, sauté diced onion and red bell pepper until softened, about 5 minutes. Next, add in a can of drained and rinsed black beans, 1/2 cup of frozen corn, cumin, smoked paprika, black pepper, and salt. Cook for another 2-3 minutes, until everything is heated through. Now, it's time to add some cheese. Stir in the cheddar cheese and Monterey Jack cheese until melted. Now it's time to assemble the empanadas. Roll out the empanada dough on a lightly floured surface to about 1/8-inch thickness. Cut the dough into 4-inch circles using a round cookie cutter or the rim of a glass. Spoon about 2 tablespoons of the black bean and corn filling onto one half of each dough circle, leaving a 1/2-inch border around the edges. Brush the beaten egg around the edges of the dough, then fold the dough over the filling to form a half-moon shape. Press the edges together to seal.

Place the empanadas on a baking sheet and brush the tops with the remaining beaten egg. Pop those bad boys in the oven and bake for 20 minutes, or until golden brown.

Serve hot, garnished with fresh chopped cilantro, or with a spicy salsa on the side. And don't forget a cold beer because these empanadas are going to be a crowd pleaser.

__Enjoy__

34. Salmon and Capers Empanadas

Prep: 15 min. Cook: 30 min. Ready In: 45 min. Servings: 4

Ingredients:

1-pound cooked salmon, flaked

1/4 cup diced onion

1/4 cup diced red bell pepper

1/4 cup diced green bell pepper

1/4 cup diced yellow bell pepper

1/4 teaspoon black pepper

1/4 teaspoon salt

1/4 cup capers

1/4 cup grated cheddar cheese

1/4 cup grated Monterey Jack cheese

1 package (15 oz) store-bought empanada dough

1 large egg, beaten with 1 tablespoon water

Cooking Directions:

Get ready for a culinary journey with these Salmon and Capers Empanadas. A unique combination of flavors that will transport you to a different place with every bite. Trust me, this recipe is worth trying. Let's get cooking!

First, preheat that oven to 375 degrees F. In a skillet, sauté diced onion, red bell pepper, green bell pepper, and yellow bell pepper until softened, about 5 minutes. Next, add in the flaked salmon, black pepper, salt, and capers. Cook for another 2-3 minutes, until everything is heated through. Now, it's time to add some cheese. Stir in the cheddar cheese and Monterey Jack cheese until melted.

Now it's time to assemble the empanadas. Roll out the empanada dough on a lightly floured surface to about 1/8-inch thickness. Cut the dough into 4-inch circles using a round cookie cutter or the rim of a glass. Spoon about 2 tablespoons of the salmon and capers filling onto one half of each dough circle, leaving a 1/2-inch border around the edges. Brush the beaten egg around the edges of the dough, then fold the dough over the filling to form a half-moon shape. Press the edges together to seal. Place the empanadas on a baking sheet and brush the tops with the remaining beaten egg. Pop those bad boys in the oven and bake for 20 minutes, or until golden brown.

Serve hot, garnished with fresh chopped parsley, or with a lemony aioli on the side. And don't forget a cold beer because these empanadas are going to be a hit.

Enjoy

35. Shrimp and Tomato Empanadas

Prep: 20 min. Cook: 20 min. Ready In: 40 min. Servings: 4

Ingredients:

1 pound of raw shrimp, peeled and deveined

1/2 cup diced onion

2 cloves of minced garlic

1/2 cup diced tomatoes

1/4 cup chopped cilantro

1/2 teaspoon smoked paprika

1/4 teaspoon cumin

Salt and pepper to taste

1 egg, beaten

Store-bought empanada dough

Cooking Directions:

Listen up folks, you want a taste of something truly special? These shrimp and tomato empanadas are where it's at. Trust me, I've traveled the world and I know my empanadas. So, fire up the stove and let's get cooking.

In a skillet, heat the olive oil over medium heat. Add the onion and garlic and cook until softened, about 5 minutes.

Add the shrimp and cook until they turn pink, about 3 minutes.

Stir in the diced tomatoes, cumin, smoked paprika, and salt. Cook for an additional 5 minutes, or until the mixture has thickened.

Remove from heat and stir in the chopped cilantro.

Preheat the oven to 375°F.

Roll out the empanada dough on a lightly floured surface.

Cut the dough into 4-inch circles.

Place about 2 tablespoons of the shrimp mixture on one half of each circle. Brush the edges with the beaten egg.

Fold the dough over the filling to form a half-moon shape and press the edges with a fork to seal.

Brush the top with the beaten egg.

Place the empanadas on a baking sheet and bake for about 20 minutes, or until golden brown.

Alright, the timer just went off and these bad boys are looking beautiful. Crispy on the outside, hot, and juicy on the inside. Perfection. Serve them up with a cold beer and enjoy. Bon appétit!

Enjoy

36. Tuna and Red Onion Empanadas

Prep: 15 min. Cook: 20 min. Ready In: 35 min. Servings: 4

Ingredients:

1 package store-bought empanada dough

1 can of tuna, drained

1/2 red onion, finely diced

1/4 cup chopped fresh cilantro

1/4 cup raisins

1/4 cup sliced green olives

1/4 teaspoon cumin

Salt and pepper

1 egg, beaten

Cooking Directions:

Empanadas, those delicious little pockets of heaven filled with all sorts of goodies. Today, we're going to be making something special, Tuna and Red Onion Empanadas. Perfect for a quick lunch or a snack, these babies are packed with flavor and easy to make. So, let's get started.

Preheat the oven to 375 degrees F (190 degrees C). Line a baking sheet with parchment paper.

Dust a clean surface with flour and roll out the empanada dough to 1/8-inch thickness.

In a medium bowl, combine the tuna, red onion, cilantro, raisins, olives, cumin, salt, and pepper.

Place a heaping tablespoon of the filling onto one half of each round of dough, leaving a 1/2-inch border around the edges.

Brush the edges of the dough with the beaten egg, then fold the dough over the filling and press the edges to seal.

Place the empanadas on the prepared baking sheet and brush the tops with the remaining egg.

Bake for 20 minutes, or until golden brown.

And there you have it folks, Tuna, and Red Onion Empanadas. These little pockets of deliciousness are perfect for any occasion, whether it's a quick lunch or a snack. So, go ahead and give them a try, and let me know what you think. Bon Appetit!

Enjoy

37. Egg and Bacon Empanadas

Prep: 15 min. Cook: 20 min. Ready In: 35 min. Servings: 4

Ingredients:

All-purpose flour for dusting

1 package store-bought empanada dough

4 eggs

4 slices of bacon, cooked and diced

1/4 cup diced onion

1/4 cup diced bell pepper

1/4 cup diced jalapeño pepper

1/4 cup shredded cheddar cheese

Salt and pepper

1 egg, beaten

Cooking Directions:

Empanadas, the ultimate comfort food. And today, we're going to be making something that's going to knock your socks off, Egg and Bacon Empanadas. These bad boys are packed with flavor and perfect for a lazy brunch or a satisfying snack. So, let's get cracking.

Preheat the oven to 375 degrees F (190 degrees C). Line a baking sheet with parchment paper. Dust a clean surface with flour and roll out the empanada dough to 1/8-inch thickness. In a medium skillet, scramble the eggs until cooked through. In a medium bowl, combine the scrambled eggs, bacon, onion, bell pepper, jalapeño pepper, cheddar cheese, salt, and pepper.

Place a heaping tablespoon of the filling onto one half of each round of dough, leaving a 1/2-inch border around the edges.

Brush the edges of the dough with the beaten egg, then fold the dough over the filling and press the edges to seal.

Place the empanadas on the prepared baking sheet and brush the tops with the remaining egg.

Bake for 20 minutes, or until golden brown.

And there you have it folks, Egg and Bacon Empanadas. Perfect for a lazy brunch or a satisfying snack, these babies are sure to please. So, go ahead and give them a try, and let me know what you think. Bon Appetit!

Enjoy

38. Turkey and Gravy Empanadas

Prep: 15 min. Cook: 30 min. Ready In: 45 min. Servings: 4

Ingredients:

All-purpose flour for dusting

1 package store-bought empanada dough

2 cups cooked turkey, diced

1/4 cup diced onion

1/4 cup diced celery

1/4 cup diced carrots

1/4 cup turkey gravy

Salt and pepper

1 egg, beaten

Cooking Directions:

Empanadas, the ultimate way to use up leftovers. And today, we're going to be making something that's going to make your Thanksgiving leftovers sing, Turkey and Gravy Empanadas. These bad boys are packed with flavor and perfect for a quick lunch or a snack. So, let's get started.

Preheat the oven to 375 degrees F (190 degrees C). Line a baking sheet with parchment paper.

Dust a clean surface with flour and roll out the empanada dough to 1/8-inch thickness.

In a medium bowl, combine the turkey, onion, celery, carrots, gravy, salt, and pepper.

Place a heaping tablespoon of the filling onto one half of each round of dough, leaving a 1/2-inch border around the edges.

Brush the edges of the dough with the beaten egg, then fold the dough over the filling and press the edges to seal.

Place the empanadas on the prepared baking sheet and brush the tops with the remaining egg.

Bake for 20 minutes, or until golden brown.

And there you have it folks, Turkey and Gravy Empanadas. These little pockets of deliciousness are the perfect way to use up those Thanksgiving leftovers. So, go ahead and give them a try, and let me know what you think. Bon Appetit!

Enjoy

39. Chicken and Cauliflower Empanadas

Prep: 15 min. Cook: 20 min. Ready In: 35 min. Servings: 4

Ingredients:

All-purpose flour for dusting

1 package store-bought empanada dough

2 cups cooked chicken, diced

1 cup cooked and mashed cauliflower

1/4 cup diced onion

1/4 cup diced bell pepper

1/4 cup diced jalapeño pepper

1/4 cup shredded cheddar cheese

Salt and pepper

1 egg, beaten

Cooking Directions:

Empanadas, a true global dish, adaptable to any flavor and ingredients. Today, we're going to be making something special, Chicken and Cauliflower Empanadas. Perfect for a quick lunch or a snack, these babies are packed with flavor and easy to make. So, let's get started.

Preheat the oven to 375 degrees F (190 degrees C). Line a baking sheet with parchment paper.

Dust a clean surface with flour and roll out the empanada dough to 1/8-inch thickness.

In a medium bowl, combine the chicken, mashed cauliflower, onion, bell pepper, jalapeño pepper, cheddar cheese, salt, and pepper.

Place a heaping tablespoon of the filling onto one half of each round of dough, leaving a 1/2-inch border around the edges.

Brush the edges of the dough with the beaten egg, then fold the dough over the filling and press the edges to seal.

Place the empanadas on the prepared baking sheet and brush the tops with the remaining egg.

Bake for 20 minutes, or until golden brown.

And there you have it folks, Chicken and Cauliflower Empanadas. These little pockets of deliciousness are perfect for any occasion, whether it's a quick lunch or a snack. So, go ahead and give them a try, and let me know what you think. Bon Appetit!

Enjoy

40. Beef and Carrot Empanadas

Prep: 30 min. Cook: 30 min. Ready In: 1 h. Servings: 4

Ingredients:

1 lb. beef chuck, cut into small cubes

1 onion, diced

3 cloves of garlic, minced

1 cup of grated carrots

1 teaspoon of paprika

1 teaspoon of cumin

1 teaspoon of salt

1/2 teaspoon of black pepper

1/2 teaspoon of dried oregano

1/4 cup of raisins

1/4 cup of green olives, sliced

1 package of store-bought empanada dough

1 egg, beaten

Cooking Directions:

Empanadas, my friends, are the ultimate street food. They're portable, delicious, and can be filled with just about anything. Today, we're going to show you how to make beef and carrot empanadas that will blow your mind. Trust me, these bad boys are worth the effort.

In a large skillet, brown the beef over medium-high heat until it's cooked through. Drain any excess fat. Add the onion and garlic to the skillet and cook until softened, about 5 minutes. Stir in the grated carrots, paprika, cumin, salt, black pepper, and oregano. Cook for an additional 5 minutes. Stir in the raisins and green olives and cook for a final 2 minutes. Remove from heat and let cool. Preheat the oven to 375 degrees F (190 degrees C). Roll out the store-bought empanada dough on a lightly floured surface. Cut into circles using a cookie cutter or a glass. Place a spoonful of the beef and carrot mixture on one half of each empanada dough circle. Brush the edges of the dough with the beaten egg. Fold the dough over the filling to create a half-moon shape and press the edges together to seal. Place the empanadas on a baking sheet and brush the tops with the remaining beaten egg.
Bake for 20-25 minutes, or until golden brown.
And there you have it, folks. Beef and carrot empanadas that will make your taste buds dance. Serve them up with some chimichurri or aioli and enjoy. Trust me, these are the real deal. Buen provecho!

Enjoy

41. Pork and Apricot Empanadas

Prep: 45 min. Cook: 30 min. Ready In: 1 h. 15 min. Servings: 4

Ingredients:

1 lb. pork shoulder, cut into small cubes

1 onion, diced

3 cloves of garlic, minced

1 cup of diced apricots

1 teaspoon of smoked paprika

1 teaspoon of cumin

1 teaspoon of salt

1/2 teaspoon of black pepper

1/4 cup of slivered almonds

1/4 cup of green olives, sliced

1/4 cup of cilantro, chopped

1 package of store-bought empanada dough

1 egg, beaten

Cooking Directions:

Empanadas, my dear friends, are the ultimate comfort food. They're warm, flaky and can be filled with just about anything. Today, we're going to show you how to make pork and apricot empanadas that will change the way you think about empanadas. Trust me, these are not your grandma's empanadas.

In a large skillet, brown the pork over medium-high heat until it's cooked through. Drain any excess fat.

Add the onion and garlic to the skillet and cook until softened, about 5 minutes. Stir in the diced apricots, smoked paprika, cumin, salt, and black pepper. Cook for an additional 5 minutes. Stir in the slivered almonds, green olives, and cilantro. Cook for a final 2 minutes. Remove from heat and let cool. Preheat the oven to 375 degrees F (190 degrees C). Roll out the store-bought empanada dough on a lightly floured surface. Cut into circles using a cookie cutter or a glass.

Place a spoonful of the pork and apricot mixture on one half of each empanada dough circle. Brush the edges of the dough with the beaten egg. Fold the dough over the filling to create a half-moon shape and press the edges together to seal. Place the empanadas on a baking sheet and brush the tops with the remaining beaten egg.

Bake for 20-25 minutes, or until golden brown.

And there you have it, folks. Pork and apricot empanadas that will make your taste buds sing. Serve them up with some chimichurri or aioli and enjoy. Trust me, these are the real deal. Buen provecho!

Enjoy

42. Black Bean and Avocado Empanadas

Prep: 30 min. Cook: 20 min. Ready In: 50 min. Servings: 4

Ingredients:

1 can of black beans, drained and rinsed

1/2 onion, diced

3 cloves of garlic, minced

1 avocado, diced

1 teaspoon of cumin

1/2 teaspoon of chili powder

1/2 teaspoon of salt

1/4 teaspoon of black pepper

1/4 cup of cilantro, chopped

1 package of store-bought empanada dough

1 egg, beaten

Cooking Directions:

Empanadas, my friends, are the epitome of versatile. They can be filled with just about anything and today we're going to show you how to make some Black Bean and Avocado Empanadas that will knock your socks off. These empanadas are not only delicious but also vegetarian and gluten-free, so you can enjoy them with no guilt, and no judgement.

In a medium skillet, sauté the onion and garlic over medium heat until softened, about 5 minutes. Stir in the black beans, avocado, cumin, chili powder, salt, and black pepper. Cook for an additional 5 minutes. Stir in the cilantro. Cook for a final 2 minutes. Remove from heat and let cool. Preheat the oven to 375 degrees F (190 degrees C). Roll out the store-bought empanada dough on a lightly floured surface. Cut into circles using a cookie cutter or a glass. Place a spoonful of the black bean and avocado mixture on one half of each empanada dough circle. Brush the edges of the dough with the beaten egg. Fold the dough over the filling to create a half-moon shape and press the edges together to seal. Place the empanadas on a baking sheet and brush the tops with the remaining beaten egg. Bake for 15-20 minutes, or until golden brown.

And there you have it, folks. Black Bean and Avocado Empanadas that will make your taste buds dance. Serve them up with some salsa or guacamole and enjoy. Trust me, these are the real deal. Buen provecho!

Enjoy

43. Salmon and Lemon Empanadas

Prep: 30 min. Cook: 20 min. Ready In: 50 min. Servings: 4

Ingredients:

1 lb. of fresh salmon fillet, skin removed and flaked

1/2 onion, diced

1/2 cup of diced red bell pepper

1/4 cup of lemon juice

1/4 cup of parsley, chopped

1 teaspoon of salt

1/4 teaspoon of black pepper

1/4 cup of grated parmesan cheese

1 package of store-bought empanada dough

1 egg, beaten

Cooking Directions:

Empanadas, my dear friends, are the ultimate party food. They're easy to make, easy to eat, and can be filled with just about anything. Today, we're going to show you how to make some Salmon and Lemon Empanadas that will make your guests ask for seconds, and maybe even thirds. Trust me, these empanadas are something special.

In a medium skillet, sauté the onion and red bell pepper over medium heat until softened, about 5 minutes. Stir in the flaked salmon, lemon juice, parsley, salt, and black pepper. Cook for an additional 2 minutes. Stir in the parmesan cheese. Cook for a final 1 minute. Remove from heat and let cool. Preheat the oven to 375 degrees F (190 degrees C). Roll out the store-bought empanada dough on a lightly floured surface. Cut into circles using a cookie cutter or a glass. Place a spoonful of the salmon and lemon mixture on one half of each empanada dough circle. Brush the edges of the dough with the beaten egg. Fold the dough over the filling to create a half-moon shape and press the edges together to seal. Place the empanadas on a baking sheet and brush the tops with the remaining beaten egg.

Bake for 15-20 minutes, or until golden brown.

And there you have it, folks. Salmon and Lemon Empanadas that will make your taste buds sing. Serve them up with some lemon wedges or tartar sauce and enjoy. Trust me, these are the real deal. Buen provecho!

Enjoy

44. Shrimp and Bell Pepper Empanadas

Prep: 30 min. Cook: 20 min. Ready In: 50 min. Servings: 4

Ingredients:

1 lb. of raw shrimp, peeled and deveined

1/2 onion, diced

1/2 cup of diced red bell pepper

1/2 cup of diced green bell pepper

1/4 cup of cilantro, chopped

1 teaspoon of cumin

1/2 teaspoon of chili powder

1/2 teaspoon of salt

1/4 teaspoon of black pepper

1/4 cup of grated queso fresco

1 package of store-bought empanada dough

1 egg, beaten

Cooking Directions:

Empanadas, my dear friends, are the ultimate party food. They're easy to make, easy to eat, and can be filled with just about anything. Today, we're going to show you how to make some Shrimp and Bell Pepper Empanadas that will impress your guests and leave them wanting more. Trust me, these empanadas are something special.

In a medium skillet, sauté the onion and bell peppers over medium heat until softened, about 5 minutes. Stir in the shrimp, cilantro, cumin, chili powder, salt, and black pepper. Cook until the shrimp are pink and cooked through, about 5 minutes. Stir in the queso fresco. Cook for a final 2 minutes. Remove from heat and let cool. Preheat the oven to 375 degrees F (190 degrees C). Roll out the store-bought empanada dough on a lightly floured surface. Cut into circles using a cookie cutter or a glass. Place a spoonful of the shrimp and bell pepper mixture on one half of each empanada dough circle. Brush the edges of the dough with the beaten egg. Fold the dough over the filling to create a half-moon shape and press the edges together to seal.

Place the empanadas on a baking sheet and brush the tops with the remaining beaten egg.

Bake for 15-20 minutes, or until golden brown.

And there you have it, folks. Shrimp and Bell Pepper Empanadas that will make your taste buds sing. Serve them up with some salsa or guacamole and enjoy. Trust me, these are the real deal. Buen provecho!

Enjoy

45. Tuna and Cucumber Empanadas

Prep: 20 min. Cook: 20 min. Ready In: 40 min. Servings: 4

Ingredients:

All-purpose flour, for dusting

1-pound store-bought empanada dough

1 can (6 ounces) tuna, drained and flaked

1/4 cup diced cucumber

1/4 cup diced red onion

1/4 cup diced red bell pepper

1/4 cup diced green bell pepper

1/4 cup diced jalapeño pepper

2 cloves garlic, minced

1/4 cup chopped fresh cilantro

1/4 cup mayonnaise

1/4 cup sour cream

1/2 teaspoon ground cumin

1/2 teaspoon smoked paprika

1/4 teaspoon salt

1/4 teaspoon black pepper

1 egg, beaten

Cooking Directions:

Empanadas are the ultimate street food, and this tuna and cucumber version is no exception. These flaky, golden-brown pockets of deliciousness are packed with flavor, and are perfect for a quick and easy lunch or dinner. And the best part? You can use store-bought dough, so you don't have to worry about making it from scratch. Let's get started.

Preheat your oven to 375°F (190°C). Line a baking sheet with parchment paper. On a lightly floured surface, roll out the empanada dough to 1/8-inch thickness.

In a medium bowl, combine the tuna, cucumber, red onion, red and green bell peppers, jalapeño, garlic, cilantro, mayonnaise, sour cream, cumin, smoked paprika, salt, and black pepper. Mix well.

Spoon about 2 tablespoons of the tuna mixture onto one half of each dough round, leaving a 1/2-inch border around the edges. Brush the edges with the beaten egg. Fold the dough over the filling, pressing the edges to seal. Crimp the edges with a fork to seal.

Place the empanadas on the prepared baking sheet. Brush the top of each empanada with the beaten egg.

Bake for 20 minutes, or until golden brown.

And there you have it, folks. Tuna and cucumber empanadas that are sure to satisfy. Serve them hot out of the oven and enjoy with a cold beer. Trust me, you won't regret it.

Enjoy

46. Egg and Ham Empanadas

Prep: 15 min. Cook: 30 min. Ready In: 45 min. Servings: 4

Ingredients:

All-purpose flour for dusting

1/2-pound cooked ham, diced

1/4 cup diced onion

1/4 cup diced red bell pepper

1/4 cup diced green bell pepper

2 cloves garlic, minced

1/4 cup chopped fresh cilantro leaves

1 tablespoon olive oil

Salt and ground black pepper to taste

1 cup shredded Monterey Jack cheese

4 large eggs, beaten

1 (15 ounce) package empanada dough or store-bought pie crust

Cooking Directions:

You know, I've always been a fan of empanadas. The flaky crust and the savory filling - it's the perfect combination of textures and flavors. And these egg and ham empanadas, well, they're a classic. They're the perfect party food, or even just a casual lunch. So, grab a beer, and let's get to work.

Preheat oven to 375 degrees F (190 degrees C).

In a large skillet, heat olive oil over medium heat. Add onion, red bell pepper, green bell pepper, and garlic. Cook and stir until vegetables are tender. Stir in cilantro. Season with salt and pepper.

Remove skillet from heat. Stir in ham and shredded cheese. Add beaten eggs and mix well.

Roll out empanada dough on a lightly floured surface to about 1/8-inch thickness. Cut into 4-inch circles.

Place a heaping tablespoon of filling on one half of each circle. Fold dough over filling, and press edges to seal. Crimp edges with a fork to ensure a tight seal.

Place empanadas on a baking sheet.

Bake in the preheated oven for 20 to 25 minutes, or until golden brown. There you have it folks, perfect egg and ham empanadas. These are best served hot, but they're also great at room temperature. So go ahead, grab one, or two, or three. And as always, enjoy your meal.

___Enjoy___

47. Chicken and Zucchini Empanadas

Prep: 15 min. Cook: 30 min. Ready In: 45 min. Servings: 4

Ingredients:

All-purpose flour for dusting

1/2-pound cooked chicken, diced

1/2 cup diced zucchini

1/4 cup diced onion

1/4 cup diced red bell pepper

1/4 cup diced green bell pepper

2 cloves garlic, minced

1/4 cup chopped fresh cilantro leaves

1 tablespoon olive oil

Salt and ground black pepper to taste

1 cup shredded Monterey Jack cheese

4 large eggs, beaten

1 (15 ounce) package empanada dough or store-bought pie crust

Cooking Directions:

Empanadas, empanadas, empanadas. I can't get enough of these tasty little pockets of goodness. And these chicken and zucchini empanadas, they're something special. The combination of tender chicken and fresh zucchini is just fantastic. So, fire up the oven and let's get to work.

Preheat oven to 375 degrees F (190 degrees C).

In a large skillet, heat olive oil over medium heat. Add onion, red bell pepper, green bell pepper, and garlic. Cook and stir until vegetables are tender. Stir in cilantro. Season with salt and pepper.

Remove skillet from heat. Stir in chicken and shredded cheese. Add beaten eggs and mix well.

Roll out empanada dough on a lightly floured surface to about 1/8-inch thickness. Cut into 4-inch circles.

Place a heaping tablespoon of filling on one half of each circle. Fold dough over filling, and press edges to seal. Crimp edges with a fork to ensure a tight seal.

Place empanadas on a baking sheet.

Bake in the preheated oven for 20 to 25 minutes, or until golden brown. And there you have it folks, chicken and zucchini empanadas. These are best served hot, but they're also great at room temperature. So go ahead, grab one, or two, or three. And as always, enjoy your meal.

Enjoy

48. Pork and Blue Berry Empanadas

Prep: 15 min. Cook: 30 min. Ready In: 45 min. Servings: 4

Ingredients:

All-purpose flour for dusting

1/2-pound cooked pork, diced

1/4 cup diced onion

1/4 cup diced red bell pepper

1/4 cup diced green bell pepper

1/2 cup fresh blueberries

2 cloves garlic, minced

1/4 cup chopped fresh cilantro leaves

1 tablespoon olive oil

Salt and ground black pepper to taste

1 cup shredded Monterey Jack cheese

4 large eggs, beaten

1 (15 ounce) package empanada dough or store-bought pie crust

Cooking Directions:

Empanadas, empanadas, empanadas. I love empanadas. The flaky crust, the savory filling. And these pork and blueberry empanadas, well they're something special. The sweetness of the blueberries and the savory pork, it's a unique and delicious combination. So, fire up the oven and let's get to work.

Preheat oven to 375 degrees F (190 degrees C).

In a large skillet, heat olive oil over medium heat. Add onion, red bell pepper, green bell pepper, and garlic. Cook and stir until vegetables are tender. Stir in cilantro. Season with salt and pepper.

Remove skillet from heat. Stir in pork, blueberries, and shredded cheese. Add beaten eggs and mix well.

Roll out empanada dough on a lightly floured surface to about 1/8-inch thickness. Cut into 4-inch circles.

Place a heaping tablespoon of filling on one half of each circle. Fold dough over filling, and press edges to seal. Crimp edges with a fork to ensure a tight seal.

Place empanadas on a baking sheet.

Bake in the preheated oven for 20 to 25 minutes, or until golden brown. And there you have it folks, pork and blueberry empanadas. Although it's not a traditional combination of ingredients, it's a unique and delicious flavor. These are best served hot, but they're also great at room temperature. So go ahead, grab one, or two, or three. And as always, enjoy your meal.

<u>Enjoy</u>

49. Black Beans and Sweet Pepper Empanadas

Prep: 15 min. Cook: 30 min. Ready In: 45 min. Servings: 4

Ingredients:

All-purpose flour for dusting

1 (15 ounce) can black beans, drained and rinsed

1/4 cup diced onion

1/4 cup diced red bell pepper

1/4 cup diced green bell pepper

1/4 cup diced sweet pepper

2 cloves garlic, minced

1/4 cup chopped fresh cilantro leaves

1 tablespoon olive oil

Salt and ground black pepper to taste

1 cup shredded Monterey Jack cheese

4 large eggs, beaten

1 (15 ounce) package empanada dough or store-bought pie crust

Cooking Directions:

Empanadas, empanadas, empanadas. I've had my fair share of these delicious pockets of goodness, and I've got to say, these black bean and sweet pepper empanadas are something special. The combination of savory black beans and sweet peppers is a classic and always a crowd pleaser. So, let's get to work and make some empanadas.

Preheat oven to 375 degrees F (190 degrees C).

In a large skillet, heat olive oil over medium heat. Add onion, red bell pepper, green bell pepper, sweet pepper, and garlic. Cook and stir until vegetables are tender. Stir in cilantro. Season with salt and pepper.

Remove skillet from heat. Stir in black beans and shredded cheese. Add beaten eggs and mix well.

Roll out empanada dough on a lightly floured surface to about 1/8-inch thickness. Cut into 4-inch circles.

Place a heaping tablespoon of filling on one half of each circle. Fold dough over filling, and press edges to seal. Crimp edges with a fork to ensure a tight seal.

Place empanadas on a baking sheet.

Bake in the preheated oven for 20 to 25 minutes, or until golden brown. And there you have it folks, black bean and sweet pepper empanadas that are sure to be a hit at any gathering. These are best served hot, but they're also great at room temperature. So go ahead, grab one, or two, or three. And as always, enjoy your meal.

Enjoy

50. Shrimp and Garlic Empanadas

Prep: 15 min. Cook: 30 min. Ready In: 45 min. Servings: 4

Ingredients:

All-purpose flour for dusting

1/2-pound cooked shrimp, peeled and deveined

1/4 cup diced onion

1/4 cup diced red bell pepper

1/4 cup diced green bell pepper

2 cloves garlic, minced

1/4 cup chopped fresh cilantro leaves

1 tablespoon olive oil

Salt and ground black pepper to taste

1 cup shredded Monterey Jack cheese

4 large eggs, beaten

1 (15 ounce) package empanada dough or store-bought pie crust

Cooking Directions:

Empanadas, empanadas, empanadas. I've had my fair share of these delicious pockets of goodness, and let me tell you, these shrimp and garlic empanadas are something special. The combination of succulent shrimp and fragrant garlic is a match made in heaven. So, let's get to work and make some empanadas.

Preheat oven to 375 degrees F (190 degrees C).

In a large skillet, heat olive oil over medium heat. Add onion, red bell pepper, green bell pepper and garlic. Cook and stir until vegetables are tender. Stir in cilantro. Season with salt and pepper.

Remove skillet from heat. Stir in shrimp and shredded cheese. Add beaten eggs and mix well.

Roll out empanada dough on a lightly floured surface to about 1/8-inch thickness. Cut into 4-inch circles.

Place a heaping tablespoon of filling on one half of each circle. Fold dough over filling, and press edges to seal. Crimp edges with a fork to ensure a tight seal.

Place empanadas on a baking sheet.

Bake in the preheated oven for 20 to 25 minutes, or until golden brown. And there you have it folks, shrimp and garlic empanadas that are sure to be a hit at any gathering. These are best served hot, but they're also great at room temperature. So go ahead, grab one, or two, or three. And as always, enjoy your meal.

Enjoy

Thank you for purchasing
Top 50 Most Delicious Empanada Recipes.

We hope you found the recipes as tasteful and delicious as we do.

Please show your support and love for empanadas by leaving a review on Amazon.

Make sure to check out all the other delicious recipes in the Top 50 Most Delicious cookbook series.